PRESENTED BY
Willard Suderman

THAT EVERYONE MAY HEAR
REACHING THE UNREACHED

THAT EVERYONE MAY HEAR

REACHING THE UNREACHED

EDWARD R. DAYTON

MARC
919 West Huntington Drive, Monrovia, California 91016
A Ministry of World Vision International

Library of Congress Number 79-88986

Copyright © 1979 by
MISSIONS ADVANCED RESEARCH AND
COMMUNICATION CENTER
A Ministry of World Vision International

All Rights Reserved

ISBN 0-912552-29-8

Printed in the United States of America

TABLE OF CONTENTS

	Page Number
PREFACE	
INTRODUCTION	
1. The Task of World Evangelization	13
2. How Do We Evangelize the World?	21
3. How Do We Find the Unreached People?	31
4. How Do We Reach the Unreached?	37
5. Discovering God's Approach: People to People	45
6. Coming to Know a People	53
7. Who Should Reach Them?	61
8. How Should They be Reached?	65
9. What Will be the Result?	69
10. For Further Help	77

PREFACE

In the fourteen years between the Congress on World Evangelism in Berlin in 1966 and the Consultation on World Evangelization at Pattaya in 1980 a great deal has happened. The missionary vitality of the Church has been renewed. The Holy Spirit has been at work among us.

We have faced up to the magnitude of the task and, confronted by what appears to be an impossible undertaking, have reconfirmed our faith in God's desire and ability to do it.

We have come to see the world in a new way, not 221 nation-states, but thousands of people groups, within which God intends His Church to take root and grow.

Through experiences, conversations, conferences, books and research we have shared with one another how the Holy Spirit is still acting in the world. We have been amazed at both His diversity and His willingness to work in thousands of different situations.

Through its various Working Groups the Lausanne Committee for World Evangelization has continued the research, discussion and fact-finding begun at the International Congress on World Evangelization held at Lausanne in 1974. It was MARC's privilege to prepare Status of Christianity Country Profiles and a directory of *Unreached Peoples* for the 1974 meeting. Since 1966 we had been working to refine the concept of seeing the world as people groups. The first edition of *Planning Strategies for Evangelism* was presented in workshops at Lausanne.

Since that time the directory of *Unreached Peoples* has become an annual publication of the David C. Cook Company, and *Planning Strategies for Evangelism* has been tested and refined into its sixth edition.

This small book is an attempt to make available to Christians all over the world a simple, but effective, approach to world evangelization.

We send it forth with the prayer that God will use it to show you where you can fit as part of His marvelous strategy.

Monrovia, California
June, 1979

INTRODUCTION

THE PURPOSE OF THIS BOOK

All over the world members of Christ's Church are gaining new insights into how to reach unreached people. As a result of the many congresses that have been held both nationally and internationally, and the outcome of thousands of hours of patient research, issuing forth from millions of hours of prayer, have come new understandings of the Holy Spirit's power to change life. This book is an attempt to summarize those results and to make them available to those whom God has called to be His evangelists to the over three billion people in the world who do not know Jesus Christ as Lord and Savior.

WHO SHOULD USE THIS BOOK?

This book is not written by those only casually interested in evangelization. Rather, it is an attempt to help those within whom God has placed an unquenchable desire to share His love and grace.

It is not a book that can be read and put aside in one day. It is designed for constant review. It is designed as a tool that the Holy Spirit can use to continually prod us to greater efforts toward world evangelization.

HOW TO USE THIS BOOK

The first half of this book attempts to help the evangelist focus in on the people to be reached. It is something that needs to be discussed, and understood and prayed over before moving on to the second half which leads us through those questions which have been found useful to help us to discover God's strategy. Although it will be very useful to individuals, it will find its greatest use when there is a small group of people, members of the same organization or the same local church, who feel God's leading towards reaching a specific people. When such a group exists, the best way to use this book is to read it individually, and then jointly view the accompanying audiovisual that has been prepared by the Strategy Working Group and MARC.

Only when there has been a thorough discussion on the whole concept of a people group and the desirability of focusing in on them specifically, should the group move on to attempting to answer the questions given in the second half of the book.

When the first half has been adequately reviewed, then we suggest that <u>as a group</u> an attempt be made to answer the questions in the second half. This can be done fairly quickly under the leadership of a group leader, writing down the answers to whatever questions are available and seeking to discover other questions. This preliminary exercise will give the group an understanding as to the magnitude of the questions and will help the Holy Spirit to present to them ideas of how they can best plan their strategy.

Again, we have to continually remind ourselves that this is not a simple process. The answers do not come easily. The questions are often more important than the answers.

Ultimately each group of evangelists should attempt to write their own set of questions and answers which reflect God's particular strategy for the group to which they have been called.

A SPECIAL EDITION

This special edition of *That Everyone May Hear* is part of a study package designed for special interest study groups that will be convening all over the world preparatory to the Consultation on World Evangelization to be held in Pattaya, Thailand, in June of 1980. These study groups are an attempt to look at unreached peoples from many and varied perspectives. Unreached peoples can be seen within the context of their religions, within their age groups, within their geographical locations, and many different ways. These study groups will be attempting to understand some of the keys that God may be designing to unlock the doors of the minds and hearts of peoples all over the world. The groups are described in Chapter 10 on pages 77 and 78.

An audiovisual covering a great deal of the material in this book is available for these study groups through their coordinators. This audiovisual has been designed to be used in conjunction with this book. The audiovisual is described in greater detail in Chapter 10 on page 79.

This book is intended to help study groups think through the particular people that God wants them to describe and plan to reach. By attempting to answer some of the questions that it contains, it is hoped that the work of the hundreds of study groups all over the world will have about them a degree of consistency that will help those that God brings together in Pattaya in June 1980 to have a better appreciation of God's strategy for world evangelization.

Both the book and the audiovisual are intended to be translated into other languages. At the time of its writing an immediate translation into Spanish was planned. For further information on what languages may already be available, please write to MARC, 919 West Huntington Drive, Monrovia, California 91016, U.S.A. Please also tell us about your plans to translate the book or the audiovisual so that we may share them with others.

1

THE TASK OF
WORLD EVANGELIZATION

The Lord Jesus Christ has commanded His Church to make disciples of every nation. This task has been given to His Church, His body. Every Christian in every local church, in every country of the world, is called upon to be a witness to the saving power of Jesus Christ.

> Jesus drew near and said to them, 'I have been given all authority in heaven and on earth. Go, then, to all peoples everywhere and make them my disciples: baptize them in the name of the Father, the Son, and the Holy Spirit' (Matthew 28:18,19, TEV).

No matter who we are and where we are, if we claim Jesus as Lord, God's command to us is that we should proclaim our faith by what we say and how we live.

And the Church is multiplying its witness around the world. On every continent men and women are gossiping the gospel to their friends, to their neighbors, to the village or city within which they live. However, in addition to these local witnesses, God has set apart certain men and women to go forth from where they live to reach those villages, towns and cities within which there is no witness. We follow in the train of those early apostles who were <u>set aside</u> for the work to which the Holy Spirit had called them.

> In the church at Antioch there were some prophets and
> teachers: Barnabas, Simeon (called the Black), Lucius
> (from Cyrene), Manaen (who had been brought up with
> Governor Herod), and Saul. While they were serving
> the Lord and fasting, the Holy Spirit said to them,
> 'Set apart for me Barnabas and Saul, to do the work
> to which I have called them' (Acts 13:1,2, TEV).

If the world is to be evangelized, if every person in the world is to have an opportunity to know Jesus Christ as Lord and Savior, then these special ambassadors, these cross-cultural missionaries, need to understand the people to whom they are called. We need to understand the people of the world as God knows them. We need to uncover God's strategy, God's plan for reaching these people.

DEFINING WORLD EVANGELIZATION

Let us begin with some definitions. What do we mean by world evangelization?:

> NATURE: The nature of evangelization is the communication of the good news.
>
> PURPOSE: The purpose of evangelization is to give individuals and groups a valid opportunity to accept Jesus Christ.
>
> GOAL: The measurable goal of evangelization is to persuade men and women to accept Jesus Christ as Lord and Savior, and serve Him in the fellowship of His Church.

We divide this definition into _nature_, _purpose_ and _goal_ so as to build a bridge between God's intention and our response. Only the Lord really knows whether a man or a woman has given true allegiance to Jesus Christ. But it is the _nature_ of evangelization that the good news, the gospel, be communicated.

It is the _purpose_ of evangelization that ultimately every individual and group of people in the world should have a valid opportunity to accept or reject Jesus Christ as Lord and Savior.

But if this is to be carried out in any meaningful way, we need a measurable _goal_. Thus we state that the _goal_ of world evangelization, the only biblical goal that we can actually observe, is that men and women should not only come to accept Jesus Christ as Lord and Savior but that they should come to serve Him in the fellowship of His Church.

THAT EVERYONE MAY HEAR

Every man and woman in the world... How do we think about the entire world? The task seems so enormous. We find few people today talking about world evangelization. Somehow that seems like too big a dream in a world that every day grows more complex, a world torn by disasters, political upheaval and starving people. Where do we begin? We might begin with population.

THE POPULATION OF THE WORLD

The population of the world continues to grow at an increasing rate. The challenge grows greater every day:

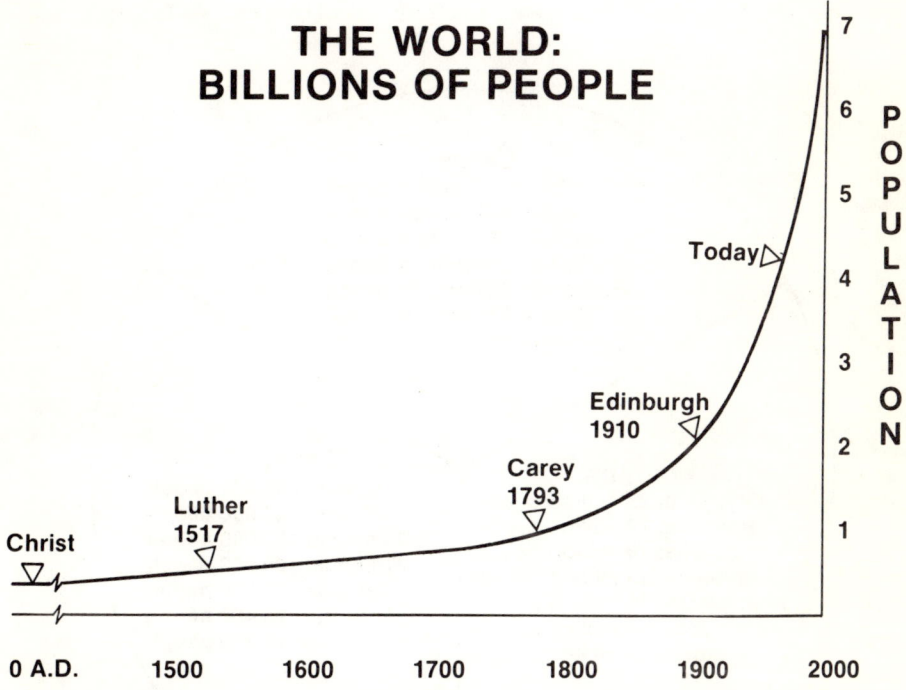

When we look at today's world population we are surprised at what has happened in such a few years. Between the time of Jesus' birth, when the population of the world was estimated at 250 million, and Martin Luther's dramatic challenge at Wittenberg, the population only doubled. It took 1500 years for the population of the world to move from 250 million to 500 million people. In 1793 William Carey, the so-called "father of modern missions," set sail for India. In a little over 250 years the population had doubled again.

By the time of the Edinburgh Missionary Conference in 1910 the population had doubled again and now stood at over two billion.

In the years since that time the population has more than doubled, and if it continues at this same rate, by the year 2000 it will be somewhere between six and seven billion people.

How do you even think about a world like that?

THE COUNTRIES OF THE WORLD

One way to think about it is in terms of the world's countries. While these are sometimes called "nation-states," we are not really talking about the nations that the Bible describes, rather we are talking about the geographical territories, political entities.

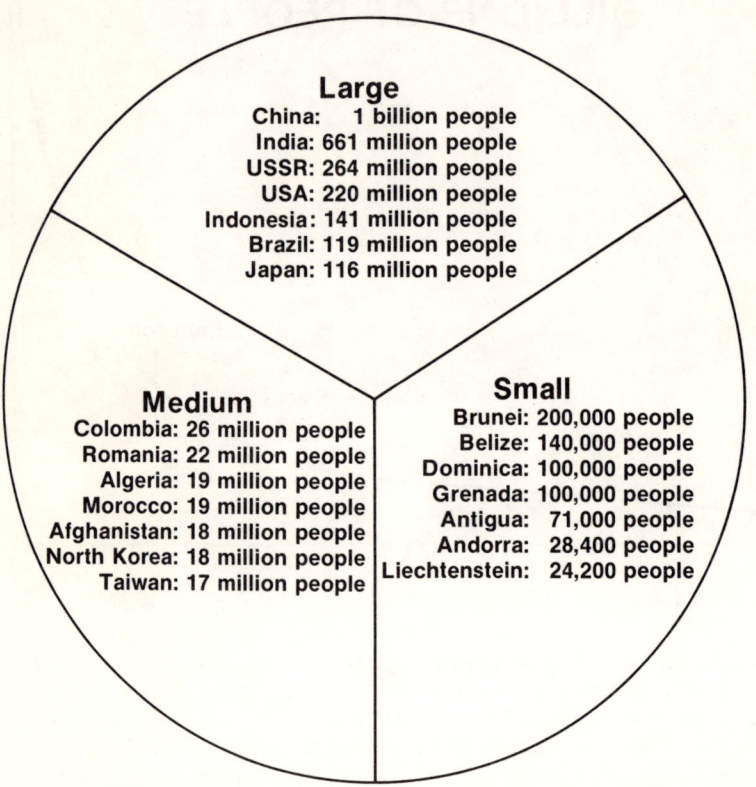

THE WORLD: 221 COUNTRIES

The 221 countries of the world come in all sizes. We have shown
them here as large, medium and small. From the estimated 1000
million people in China they dwindle down to the mere 23,700
people in Liechtenstein. That tremendous variation shows how
difficult it is to talk about world evangelization in terms of
countries. It is one thing to evangelize Liechtenstein. It is
quite another to reach the 136 million people of the many-
islanded-country of Indonesia.

THE RELIGIONS OF THE WORLD

Another way to think about the world is in terms of its religions:

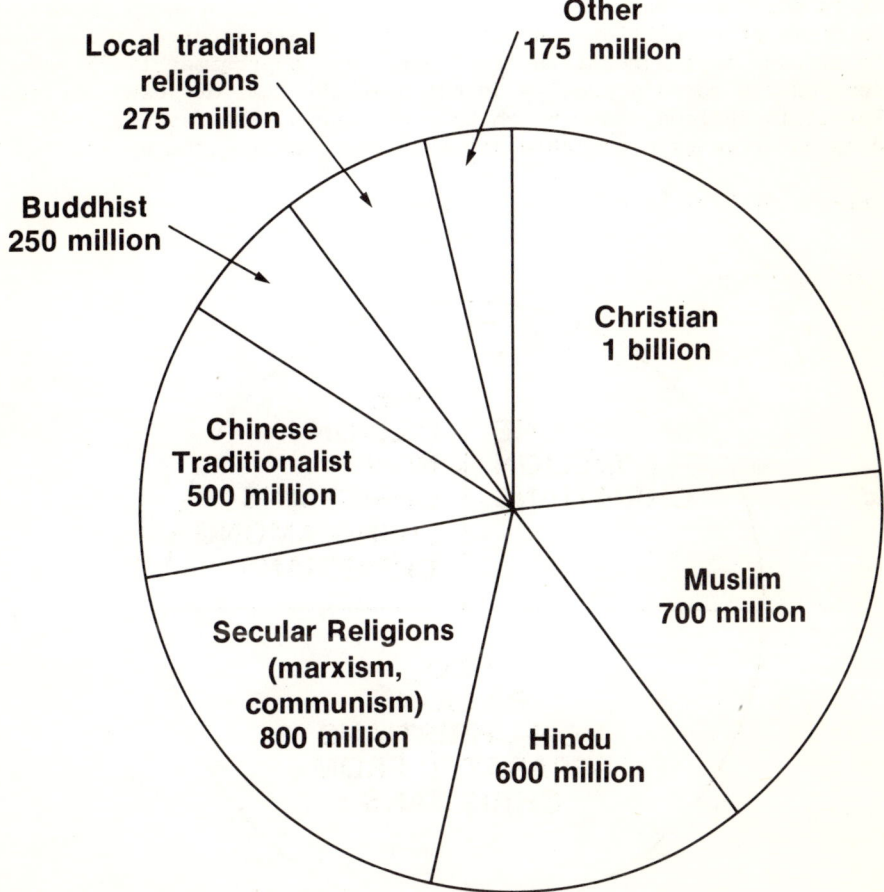

THE WORLD: ITS RELIGIONS

Christians, those who acknowledge Jesus Christ as Lord, number approximately one billion people. The second largest religion in the world is Islam, with an estimated 700 million Muslims. The 600 million Hindus are found all over the world, with the majority in India.

Secular religions (such as Marxism and Communism) include approximately 800 million people.

Chinese traditionalists are estimated to be 500 million. There are 250 million Buddhists in the world and 275 million traditional religionists, those who worship nature or the spirit world. Traditional Japanese, 15 million Jews and all of the other religions of the world make up the balance.

It is not important as to how accurate any of these numbers are. In terms of proportions and magnitude they are accurate enough to give us a picture of the challenge that approximately 75 percent of the world's peoples do not name the name of Jesus Christ. But it is obvious that though this breakdown helps us, it still does not give us a workable strategy for reaching the world.

But the problem is even more complex.

THE CHALLENGE

THE CHALLENGE

What we have tried to show in this figure is that of the approximate three billion people who are not Christians, only one-third or one billion, live within a culture where there are Christians who know Jesus and can share His love. To put that in reverse, no matter how earnest all of the local churches in the world were to reach out to their neighbors, only one-third of the non-Christians in the world could be reached by Christians who speak their language and understand their culture.

Such people are not only unreached, they are living in places around the world where no Christians see them. They are <u>hidden</u> people. We need to say it over and over.

There are over TWO BILLION HIDDEN PEOPLE.

> But how can they call to him for help if they have not believed? And how can they believe if they have not heard the message? And how can they hear if the message is not proclaimed? And how can the message be proclaimed if the messengers are not sent out? As the scripture says, 'How wonderful is the coming of messengers who bring good news!' (Romans 10:14,15, TEV).

2

HOW DO WE EVANGELIZE THE WORLD?

HOW DO YOU REACH A WORLD LIKE THAT?

- Not One Country At A Time

- Not One Religion At A Time

- Not One Person At A Time

- ONE PEOPLE AT A TIME

Not one country at a time, because countries vary so much. India, with its 661 million people, has 17 official languages and 400 scheduled castes. Certainly the reaching of India is quite a different task than the reaching of Andorra with its 29,200 people.

Not one religion at a time. Not only are most of the major religions of the world huge in number, they are also spread out through all of the different peoples of the world.

Not one person at a time. As we have already tried to show, the ability of individuals who are already Christians to reach the rest of the world without some cross-cultural training and understanding is not adequate to do the job.

ONE PEOPLE AT A TIME is the way to do it.

WHAT IS A PEOPLE?

> A PEOPLE--A significantly large sociological grouping of individuals who perceive themselves to have a common affinity for one another.
>
> Because of their shared:
>
> Language
>
> Religion
>
> Ethnicity
>
> Residence
>
> Occupation
>
> Class or caste
>
> Situation
>
> Etc.
>
> Or combinations of these.

The definition may seem rather filled with scientific jargon when one first reads it. Let's break it apart and look at it.

But before doing that, let's try to define what we mean by stating what we do <u>not</u> mean. By a people we do not <u>necessarily</u> mean a tribal group. By a people we do not <u>necessarily</u> mean all of the people living within a country.

When we think of a people, we try to think of them the way God sees them, or to put it another way, to understand them <u>in terms of reaching them</u> with the gospel. We are attempting to define the world <u>in terms of world evangelization</u>.

By "significantly large" we mean a group usually large enough to believe that it is a group. It might be 100. It might be a million.

By "sociological grouping of individuals" we mean people who are relating to one another in a particular situation. They may live in the same place, have the same occupation, or be of the same class or caste.

"Who perceive themselves" needs some further defining. People who speak the same language would obviously perceive themselves as having a common affinity. People who are of the same ethnic background would see themselves the same way. But the people who are in the same situation, even though they may not closely relate to one another on a day-by-day basis, can also perceive

themselves in the same group. For example, people who live in a
high-rise apartment in New York City may know one another as a
group of strangers, as individuals. Yet in their individuality,
and their statements about themselves, they see themselves as
part of a group, which, from the view of world evangelization, has
a commonness about it. There is "a common affinity for one
another."

Now this sociological grouping, this perception, this common
affinity, can be based on a lot of things. We have listed language, religion, ethnic background, where they live, business
or occupation they have, the class or caste to which they belong,
or anything about the situation which they are in, or any combination of these.

>   EXAMPLES: Urdu-speaking Muslim farmers of the Punjab

>   Cantonese-speaking Chinese refugees from Vietnam in France

>   Welsh working class miners

>   Tamil-speaking Indian workers on Malaysian rubber plantations

>   White, swinging singles in North American apartments

Perhaps our examples make the point. Notice the "boundaries"
that they place around a particular people:

Not just <u>Urdu-speaking</u> people. Not just Urdu-speaking <u>Muslims</u>,
but Urdu-speaking Muslim <u>farmers</u> who happen to live in the Punjab.

There are lots of <u>Cantonese-speaking</u> Chinese. There are fewer
of them who are <u>refugees</u>. The people we are describing here are
Cantonese-speaking refugees <u>from Vietnam</u> who right now are <u>living
in France</u>.

To speak of evangelizing <u>Wales</u> is one thing. To speak of evangelizing the <u>working class</u> of Wales would narrow it down some. But
to speak of evangelizing the Welsh working class <u>miners</u> gets much
more specific and defines a people group.

Every country is filled with such people groups. At first glance
we may believe that all the people in our country are "just like
us." But closer examination will show a vast mosaic of differ-
ences. Take, for example, the City of Greater Los Angeles. Since
this is a major city in the western part of the United States, at

first glance one might think that all of the people who live in Los Angeles are probably white and speak English. We might imagine that some would be Roman Catholics or Protestants, while a few might be Jewish. However, most people outside of Los Angeles would not expect too much diversity beyond that.

However, when we examine the 7,084,000 people of Los Angeles County more closely they look like this.

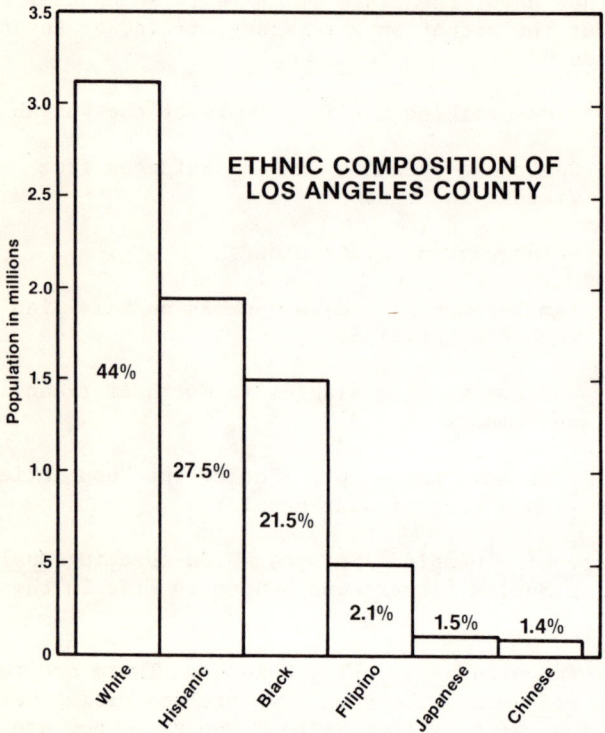

Our graph shows only the ethnic make-up of Los Angeles. Within this vast mosaic are many sub-groups defined by local neighborhoods, occupations, age and many other factors.

Los Angeles is just one example. Your country is very much the same. Think about your own country, province or state for a moment. What kind of people groups do you see who live around you, people who are different in some way than you are? Look at the example on page 25, and then write down the people you see around you on page 26.

REACHING THE UNREACHED PEOPLES IN __Brazil__
(country, state, province)

SON OF MAN, WHAT DO YOU SEE?				"...SON OF MAN, CAN THESE BONES LIVE?..." Ezekiel 37:3	
Name of Group	Where are They Located?	How Many People In This Group?	Their Present Religion	What Do You Know About Them?	How Can They Best Be Reached?
Bororo	Rural Mato Grosso	500	Animism	Also called Coroado. Bible translators in tribe. Bible portions translated in 1972. Semi-isolated.	Brazilian Christians might be good witnesses. Literacy classes could be helpful.
Japanese Immigrants	Main cities, some rural areas	750,000	Buddhism	Among middle-class people in various occupations. Easy to reach. Scriptures available. At least 15 church groups have Japanese congregations.	Evangelists should know Japanese traditional literature. Radio and home visits can help. Sacred gospel. Some interest among young people.
Yanomam	Roraima region; also in Venezuela	3000	Animism	Also called Vaica. Semi-nomadic, lower class group. Gospel portions translated. One mission agency working.	Personal and small group evangelism. Literacy training.

25

REACHING THE UNREACHED PEOPLES IN _____
(country, state, province)

	SON OF MAN, WHAT DO YOU SEE?			"...SON OF MAN, CAN THESE BONES LIVE?..." Ezekiel 37:3	
Name of Group	Where are They Located?	How Many People in This Group?	Their Present Religion	What Do You Know About Them?	How Can They Best Be Reached?

Some of these people are reached. Some are not reached.

WHAT IS AN UNREACHED PEOPLE?

There is not much point in trying to reach any one of these groups who are already reached. But how do we define unreached? The Strategy Working Group has adopted as a working definition:

> An unreached people is a group that is less than 20 percent practicing Christian.

By this we mean that if one set up some measurement, such as church attendance, one would discover that these people were trying to live out their Christianity. What do we mean by practicing? Whatever you mean! How Christians will work out their religion in different places of the world will differ tremendously. The gospel has a marvelous ability to come into a culture and express Christ's love. Committed Christians within a particular group will know quite easily who are the practicing Christians and who are not.

WHY 20 PERCENT?

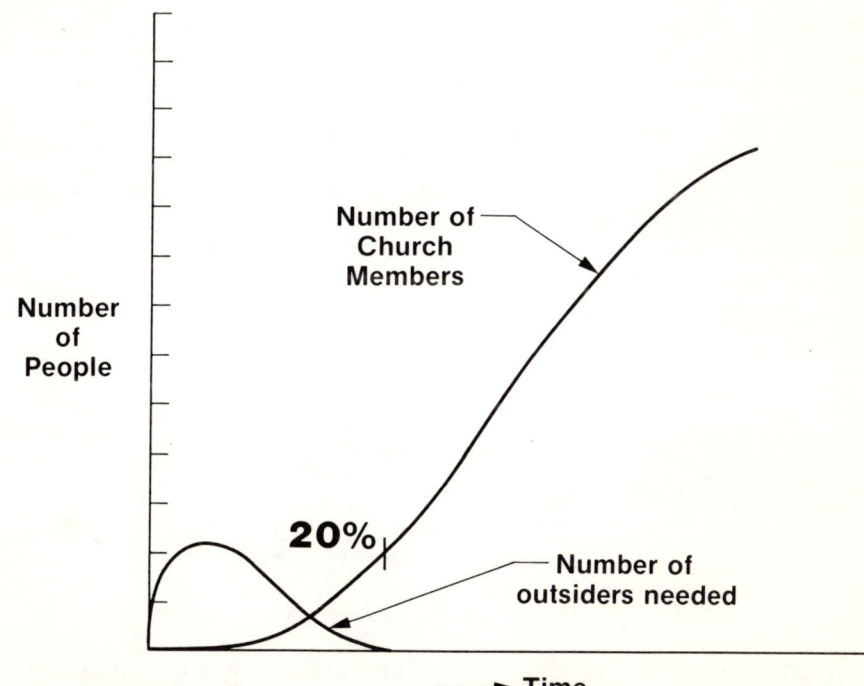

Why do we define an unreached people as "less than 20 percent of practicing Christians?" Why not ten percent or five percent or one percent? In the graph above we have shown the growth of the church within a particular group. Starting at the left with no Christians we show it growing more rapidly as time goes on. The smaller graph shows the number of cross-cultural missionaries needed. This may be a few, or it may be a large number. However, the numbers that are needed, the number of "outsiders," should decrease as the number of Christians increases. We show this number as becoming zero at 20 percent. The 20 percent figure has been chosen arbitrarily to be on the safe side. When a group is completely unreached, when there are no Christians, then someone from the "outside," someone from another culture, must attempt to bring the gospel to them. If the seed so faithfully sown falls on fertile ground, a new church will be formed. However, the missionary cannot just leave this church to its own devices. Like a mother with a newborn child, the new children in Christ need the encouragement of older and more mature Christians. But eventually the church must stand on its own feet and get on with the business of evangelizing its own people. The amount of assistance from others outside this people group must decrease.

It is estimated that when 20 percent of the people are Christians, the church within the group no longer needs any help from the outside. For all intents and purposes this group is no longer "unreached." To put it another way the reached group of people is one that is _more_ than 20 percent Christian.

But regardless of the definition, there is a vast array of unreached peoples to be reached. Some people have estimated there are between 15,000 and 25,000 major people groups who are not only unreached but who are hidden people. There are no Christians in their midst! Here are some examples of some hidden and partially reached peoples:

200,000	Turkana in Northern Kenya
50,000	Racetrack dwellers in the U.S.
1,000,000	High rise residents in Singapore
300,000	Indians in South Africa
1,200,000	Turkish laborers in Germany
30,000,000	Ajlaf Muslim farmers in Bangladesh

The world that we are concerned with is the world of unreached people. Some of these groups are large. Some are small.

EACH PEOPLE GROUP IS UNIQUE

Each group requires a unique strategy.

Each group requires a unique group of missionaries.

Each requires a special combination of evangelistic methods.

The point is that we need to <u>discover God's strategies</u>, His best way for reaching these people. Certainly if the God of the universe is capable of being concerned with <u>each individual</u> in the world, He is just as concerned for the <u>peoples</u> of the world.

WORLD EVANGELIZATION IS IN SIGHT

To think about the world in terms of reaching three billion is more than most minds can comprehend.

To think about reaching 700 million Muslims seems like an impossible task.

But when we think about the world as divided up into people groups, approximately 25,000 of which are unreached, then we have a manageable strategy. Then the Holy Spirit can help us to believe it is possible to take the whole gospel to the whole world. For if the Church is planted within each one of these people groups, it then will have the potential to reach the group of which it is a part. We need to trust God to allow us to plant a church in every people group of the world.

Go back to the chart on page 26. Are there not people groups right near you that God wants to reach through you?

3

HOW DO WE FIND THE UNREACHED PEOPLE?

HOW DO WE FIND THE UNREACHED?

- Country Profiles by LCWE Strategy Working Group

- Unreached People Surveys

- Researchers in many countries

- Correspondents around the world

- Congresses and Conferences

- Look around us

<u>Country Profiles</u>. As of July 1979 the Strategy Working Group was working on 102 countries of the world, compiling Status of Christianity Profiles. They have listed 2928 unreached people groups. These country profiles are computer compiled and stored for ease of availability and updating. Each profile contains five sections: a description of the country, a description of the people of the country, a description of the church within the country, a description of the force for evangelism attempting to reach the people within the country and a general analysis of the status of Christianity.

These country profiles are available to you in individual form or by areas. See pages 79 and 80 for more information.

Compiled in a journal known as *World Christianity*, the following areas are presently available or planned:

World Christianity

Name	Date Available
Middle East	June 11, 1979
Eastern Asia	August 31, 1979
South Asia	November 30, 1979
Latin America	February 29, 1980

Unreached peoples surveys are carried out as part of the status of Christianity research using a survey questionnaire developed by MARC and the Strategy Working Group. A computer program is used to store the information as it is received on these questionnaires. The questionnaire used is reproduced on page 85.

The Strategy Working Group has compiled an annual directory, the first of which is entitled *Unreached Peoples '79*. This directory, which is edited by Edward R. Dayton and C. Peter Wagner of the Strategy Working Group, contains an introduction which covers most of the material in this report, major articles on missiology, five case studies on what God is doing in reaching unreached people around the world, 90 descriptions of unreached peoples, a directory of unreached peoples of the world broken down by country, language, resistance/receptivity, and type of group, and a complete index of all unreached peoples which will be cumulative for future editions. This is a typical page from the directory.

On the next page we have reproduced a typical page from the directory. It gives the basic statistics on this particular group, Chinese in the United Kingdom, and then narrative background information to help with an overall understanding.

```
CHINESE IN UNITED KINGDOM                    marc id:   1225

pop:          105,000
distinct:     occupation
              ethnicity
              economic status

languages:                        uses      speak     read
              Cantonese            V         nc        nc
              Mandarin             V         nc        nc
              English              TS        nc        nc

scripture:    Bible

rlg chg:      indifferent
att chr:      somewhat favorable

religion:                         adherents
              Roman Catholic       1%
              Protestant           2%
              Traditional Chinese  60%
              Secularism           37%

churches:                         community
              Chinese Oseas. Chr. Msn.   2,000
              Roman Catholic             nc

profile:      3% No awareness
              7% Aware of existence
             75% Some knowledge of gospel
              8% Understand the message
              3% Personal challenge
              1% Decision
              2% In a fellowship
              1% Propagators of the gospel
```

As is true of the Chinese in Europe, the Chinese of England are heavily involved in the restaurant business (the heaviest concentration found in the London area). Approximately 95 percent are so employed, with three percent in nursing and two percent in other trades such as export-import, leatherwear, banking, and grocery. Most of the restaurant people speak their own Chinese dialect, but also have learned English in order to run their business.

Their distinctive occupational situation creates a problem in reaching into the some 2,000 restaurants and grills with the gospel. They have long working hours, usually from 10 a.m. until midnight, with a break of three hours in the afternoon. It is tiring and strenuous work. Workers normally have a day off, taken in turn from Monday to Thursday, but not on weekends when business is good. It is difficult to find a common time, except in afternoon break hours, when workers can gather as a group for worship or study.

Most of the restaurant workers have lesser degrees of education than the intellectuals and professionals that are also found in England. Salary is high. Social gatherings are normally with other Chinese people. While most of them claim to be Buddhists, the actual "religion" seems to be secularism and a concern for economic advancement. Concern for ancestors remains strong.

Receptivity has been higher among the nurses and professional groups that are the smallest percentage of the Chinese population. If the restaurant workers are to be reached, it will require a new approach, persons who are restaurant owners or workers themselves would be the best persons to do the evangelism.

This is the basic ongoing resource for all of those concerned with reaching the world with the good news of Jesus Christ. *Unreached Peoples '80* emphasizes unreached people among Muslims. Over 2000 unreached peoples groups are identified. *Unreached Peoples '81* is planned to focus on the peoples of Asia.

Look around us. All around us are unreached people. They are not difficult to find once one starts looking. We can look up unreached peoples in our country in the *Unreached Peoples* directory. But we can just as easily look at the fields white for harvest all around us. Look at the chart on page 26 and see what God can show you about unreached people in your city, area, state, province or region.

Researchers in many countries are making significant contributions. In addition to the work being done by MARC and the Strategy Working Group, other Christian researchers are making major contributions to this work. One of the most notable of these is the Unit of Research under the direction of Dr. David B. Barrett. Dr. Barrett is the senior editor of the forthcoming *World Christian Handbook*, work for which collaborators all over the world have been cooperating since 1968. The information gathered on Christian churches of all ecclesiastical traditions and persuasions, as well as the religions of the world, comprises a very large databank which will be the foundation for future studies in world evangelization for years to come.

Correspondents around the world form a vast network of those supplying information about unreached people. Most of the research done by the Strategy Working Group is eventually checked out with people within the countries from which the information comes.

Congresses and conferences are a major input to the task of world evangelization. The first modern day evangelical congress on world evangelization was held in Berlin in 1966. This was followed by regional and national conferences and congresses all over the world. The second major congress was the International Congress on World Evangelization, held at Lausanne in 1974, out of which the work of the Strategy Working Group has proceeded. At the time of this writing large numbers of unreached peoples conferences are being convened through area coordinators to identify and discuss strategies for reaching unreached people. All of this information will be channelled into the 1980 Consultation on World Evangelization to be held at Pattaya, Thailand, in June 1980.

4

HOW DO WE REACH THE UNREACHED?

Once we have discovered an unreached people to whom we believe God has called us, how do we reach them?

HOW DO WE REACH THEM?

THROUGH THEIR NEED:

- By trying to know them as God knows them.

- By attempting to meet their need as they see it.

- By communicating the saving power of Jesus Christ in their language and in their cultural understanding and in terms of where they are.

- By designing an overall strategy especially for them.

Western evangelism has often been carried out by people who had a solution and were looking for a problem. In other words, they assumed that there was one particular evangelistic method that would be appropriate in every setting. Evidently, God has not ordained it so. God's great love for humanity is expressed by His willingness to accept people wherever He finds them.

WHERE IS THIS PEOPLE IN
THEIR MOVEMENT TOWARD CHRIST?
The Engel Scale

```
      No Awareness of Christianity  -7
  Awareness of the Existence of Christianity  -6
        Some Knowledge of the Gospel  -5
      Understanding of the Fundamentals
                        of the Gospel  -4
        Grasp of the Personal Implications  -3
              Recognition of Personal Need  -2
     Challenge and Decision to Receive Christ  -1
                     —Conversion—
              Evaluation of the Decision  +1
   Incorporation into a Fellowship of Christians  +2
          Active Propagators of the Gospel  +3
```

This scale was originally proposed by Dr. James Engel of the Wheaton Graduate School.

This scale is not special to or peculiar to religion or Christianity. All of us, in making major decisions, go through some steps like this. And if we think back on our own conversion experience, we will discover that there were different people, different situations that "moved us" toward Christ.

There was a day when, either because of ignorance or because of our extreme youth, we had absolutely no awareness of Christianity (-7 on this scale).

Most Westerners are aware or have some awareness of Christianity (-6 on our scale), and most Americans therefore have some knowledge of the gospel (-5). The day came when we had an understanding of the fundamentals of the gospel (-4). What happened next and in what sequence was very difficult to tell. It varies tremendously from individual to individual. But in addition to this intellectual understanding, each of us has to understand that this gospel was meant for us, we have to grasp the personal implications (-3). But even that is not enough. We must also have a recognition of personal need (-2) which we think the gospel can meet. It is then that we are ready to have a challenge and decision to receive Christ (-1). What takes place next is, in purely religious terms, called "conversion." In more biblical terms we would call it regeneration, a new birth.

But as is the case in most major decisions, there is almost always an evaluation of the decision (+1). Research has shown that this is a key time in the life of a new Christian. How we minister to a person or group as they go through this evaluation has a major impact on their future.

Once this decision is past people move on to being incorporated into a fellowship of Christians (+2) and then become active propagators (+3).

We have described this decision-making process in terms of individuals. Actually, groups of people go through this same type of group process. And it is for this reason that this scale is useful to us. Let's look at some examples:

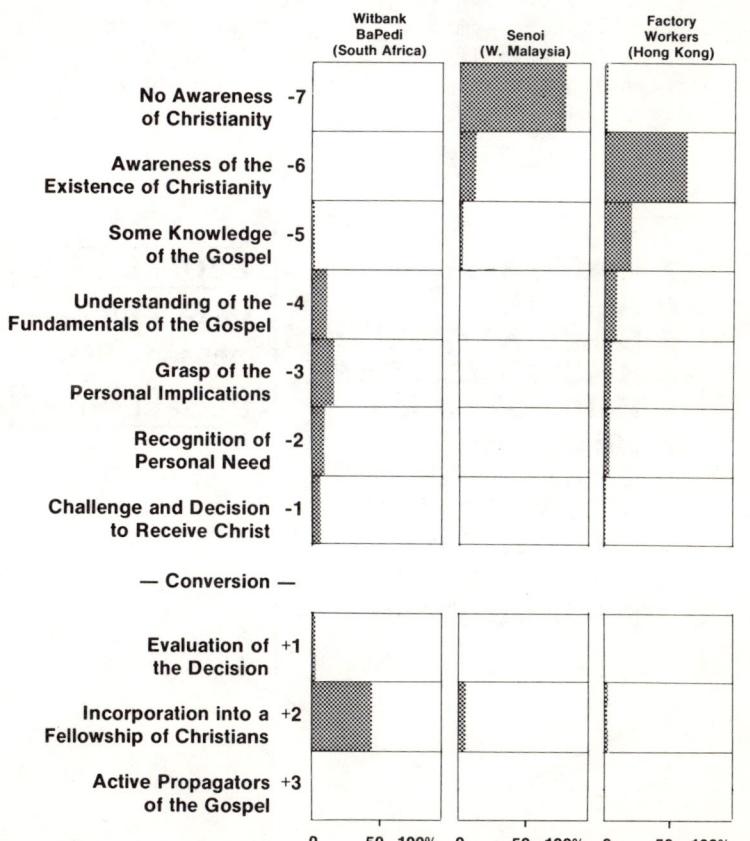

Here are three different groups of people, Witbank BaPedi in South Africa, the Senoi in West Malaysia and factory workers in Hong Kong. (Note that although these scales give the appearance of considerable precision, with the exception of the number of people who are actually Christians, these are at best rough estimates.) But as we shall see they are very useful.

The first group in our illustration are almost all Christians. Only a small percentage are still back in that category of having not moved beyond some knowledge of the gospel (-5). Approximately 45 percent of them have been incorporated into a fellowship of Christians (+2). This is a reached people.

The Senoi are at the other extreme. As best we can tell, about 80 percent of them are absolutely unaware of any existence of Christianity. True, there is a very small church (+2) but there is very little movement towards Christ.

The factory workers of Hong Kong, on the other hand, are surrounded by Christian symbols. Large numbers of them have an awareness of Christianity (-6). But the church is very small, although it appears that there are numbers of people moving towards Christ.

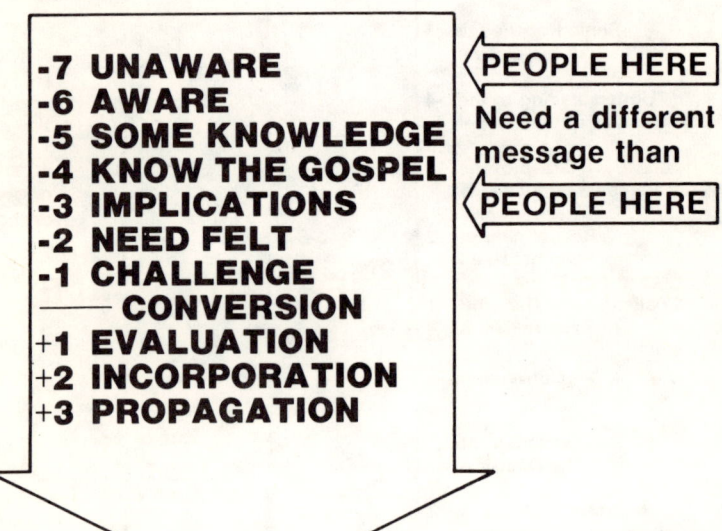

Now the advantage of these descriptions of people is that it helps us to <u>tailor our message</u>. It is not our intention to <u>change</u> the message. Rather we need to communicate it in a way that will be both understood and responded to. For example, people who have never heard of Christ, may need to know the story of God's creation in Genesis as an undergirding. People who are continually faced with the powers of the spirit world may need to be confronted with the power of the Holy Spirit. It is much like the understanding that is needed by a manufacturer of a product or a provider of a service. They have to know where the people are in order to do a good job of marketing. In the best sense of the word we want to be outstanding marketers of the gospel!

But there is still another indicator that is helpful for us to know:

RESISTANT OR RECEPTIVE?

Missionary research all over the world has shown us that there are many indicators of a people's potential receptivity or resistance to the gospel. For example, we know that people who are undergoing a great deal of economic stress, or upheavals in their way of life, are open at that time to a new understanding of the world.

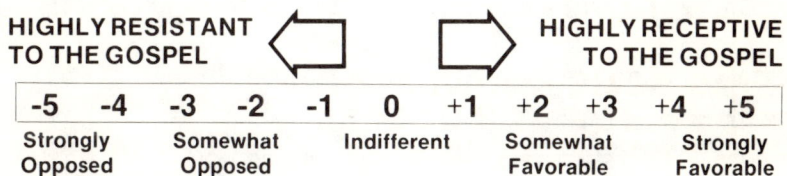

RESISTANCE/RECEPTIVITY SCALE

<u>The resistance/receptivity scale</u> helps us to know how much difficulty we are going to have in order to reach a particular people. Although it is a generalization, we can say that people who are highly receptive will probably respond to almost any evangelistic method, while people who are highly resistant are going to need a great deal of special care.

There are tremendous opportunities for the gospel around the world! Here are a few:

PEOPLE KNOWN TO BE OPEN TO THE GOSPEL

Country	Group	Population	Percent Christian
NIGERIA	AFO	25,000	1%
MALAYSIA	MELANAU OF SARAWAK	61,000	1%
PAKISTAN	SINDHIS	4,000,000	1%
INDONESIA	SUNDANESE	20,000,000	1%
SIERRA LEONE	TEMNE	1,000,000	6%
NIGERIA	BABUR THALI	75,000	5%
PERU	QUECHUA	275,000	6%
UPPER VOLTA	BUSANSE	75,000	5%
PAPUA NEW GUINEA	BANARO	2,500	8%
MALAYSIA	TAMIL PLANTATION WORKERS	137,150	1%
LIBERIA	KRAHN	250,000	9%
COLOMBIA	PAEZ	40,000	1%
ETHIOPIA	SHANKILLA	20,000	1%

This is just a <u>partial</u> list of the peoples that have been researched and recorded from all over the world. What excuse do we have in the face of this kind of information?! Yet, in the main, there are few missionaries attempting to reach these people!

5

DISCOVERING GOD'S APPROACH: PEOPLE TO PEOPLE

REACHING THE UNREACHED

The previous pages have attempted to show us how we might discover God's strategy for reaching a particular people. The rest of this book is in the form of a workbook. It has questions that are designed to help you discover your role in God's strategy for the evangelization of a specific people group.

The approach that follows is certainly not the only way to think about the glorious task of spreading the good news of the gospel throughout the world. But it <u>is</u> one way, and we think that you will discover it is applicable to Christians all over the world who are involved in sharing Christ's love with men and women who are lost without Him.

We begin with the reality that <u>God has special messengers</u> for reaching specific people. Paul was God's messenger to Gentile peoples. Peter and other apostles were sent to the Jewish groups. God goes about reaching people in many different ways. People groups are different. Individuals are different. You are a special person. The group you are trying to reach is special.

There are peoples all over the world who are "locked out" from the gospel, they are hidden people, because no one has really found a key to open the door of their understanding to Christ's love for them. They will be reached only when they are approached as unique people groups with their own culture and sense of unity.

With God's help you can design keys which will unlock the door for a particular people to whom God has called you.

But as we attempt to think God's thoughts after Him, we need to always remember one thing. The Bible is as much concerned with what we _are_ as with what we do. It is of infinite importance that men and women come to know Jesus Christ. It is of urgent importance that we have a concern to communicate the love of God to people in whatever circumstances we find them. But it is just as important that the evangelist as a person be what God wants him or her to be. To put it another way, in God's eyes who we are and how we go about telling other people of His love is just as important as how many people come to know Him as a result of our efforts.

> So then, my brothers, because of God's great mercy to us, I make this appeal to you: Offer yourselves as a living sacrifice to God, dedicated to his service and pleasing to him. This is the true worship that you should offer. Do not conform outwardly to the standards of this world, but let God transform you inwardly by a complete change of your mind. Then you will be able to know the will of God--what is good, and is pleasing to him, and is perfect (Romans 12:1,2, TEV).

GOD WANTS US TO PLAN FOR EVANGELIZATION

In the following pages we will discuss planning for evangelization. We will be asking what people does God want us to reach? What is this people like? Who should reach them? How should they reach them? What will be the result of reaching them?

Why plan for evangelization? Why not just go and be faithful servants?

> A man's mind plans his ways, but the Lord directs his steps (Proverbs 16:9, RSV).

Planning for evangelization under the Lord's direction is a powerful tool. It provides the Lord with the opportunity to direct our steps in new and creative directions. It forces us to put our faith into action, transforming our desires to see people come to know Christ into specific actions.

The world is not growing simpler or more homogeneous. In fact, it grows more complex every day. New people groups come into existence and old groups split into sub-groups as they grow larger. The task God has given us to evangelize the world demands our fervent prayer, our careful understanding and plans, and our continual sharing of the love of Christ. In the same way that each individual is precious in the sight of God and deserves personal and special attention, so each <u>group</u> of people deserves the same type of loving care.

We need to emphasize the <u>people</u> we are trying to reach. We need to take our eyes off ourselves and our methods and direct them toward the goals that God would have us reach by doing our thinking, our homework and our planning <u>before</u> we begin.

Why plan?

- Because it focuses our attention on groups of people who are unreached.

- Because it makes room for God to guide us into more effective evangelization.

- Because it shows us what we need to know and do in order to fulfill God's calling for the evangelization of a particular people.

HOW TO PROCEED

This study can be done by an individual or by groups. In either case, you will have to decide which unevangelized or unreached people you are going to try to reach. If you use it in a group, you will want all to participate in sharing what they know and think ought to be done. As suggestions are given, they can be written down as you go. <u>But the most important step is to decide on the people group to be evangelized</u>.

As best you or your group can, answer the suggested questions for each of the five steps.

You can go through the above process very quickly on the basis of what you now know, thus using these pages as a training aid. Or, you can use them to collect very specific data on peoples you are trying to reach that will help you to see your way through to understanding God's strategy and your role as part of that strategy.

<u>Don't be discouraged</u> by your lack of information! Use what you do know to help you learn more.

QUESTIONS ARE MORE IMPORTANT THAN ANSWERS

Throughout the pages that follow, we have given you numbers of questions that experience has shown the Holy Spirit can use to guide you into a better understanding. It is not important that we have the <u>answers</u> for all these questions. What is important is that in the asking of them we allow God to guide us into new understanding. And as we ask them of each other, we can sense how the Holy Spirit is moving in our midst to give us a competent understanding of how to move forward.

THE MYSTERY OF EVANGELIZATION

Planning strategies for evangelization is no substitute for the powerful presence and action of the Holy Spirit! If anything, the more carefully and prayerfully we try to think through the evangelization of a specific group, the more keenly we feel our dependence upon God.

There is a <u>mystery</u> to evangelization. The Spirit moves as He sees fit (John 3:8). It is God who is at work to do His perfect will. In ways that we cannot understand He uses imperfect, sinful men or women to communicate His love and the good news of salvation through His beloved Son to all who will receive Him.

There is a <u>mystery</u> to what happens as the Holy Spirit transforms lives of individuals and nations. We can many times see only the <u>results</u> of the Spirit's work. The finger of God writes across the pages of history, and we can see what He has done. But so often we are unable to fully understand what has happened.

But there is <u>mystery</u> too in the fact that God has charged His Church to go into all the world to preach and make disciples, trusting Him for results and yet at the same time praying, dreaming, anticipating, longing into the future. And as we respond to the command of God's word and the prompting of His Spirit within us, we are expected to bring our <u>total being</u> to bear on the task before us, to think, to pray, and to plan. Jesus spoke to the point when He said that a man should not start to build a tower or engage an enemy without first considering the possible outcomes (Luke 14:28). It was said of the early Church that they outlived, outdied, and out-thought the Roman Empire.

There is a <u>mystery</u> about God's action in society through the society itself. Many times God uses changes in the society to prepare people to receive His word.

Finally, there is <u>mystery</u> about the person of the evangelist. The Word of God has as much to say about what we are to <u>be</u> as what we are to <u>do</u>. The gospel is proclaimed through the spoken word. People cannot come to a knowledge of the Savior unless they hear (or read) that He is. But they are often attracted to Him by the love they find among His disciples.

Remember, each disciple is called upon to see himself or herself as part of a larger body (1 Corinthians 12:12). Within that body each has a special place and in the process of evangelization different persons play their special role at different times. "I sowed, Apollos watered, but God gave the increase" (1 Corinthians 3:6, RSV).

Let us then use <u>all</u> the gifts that God has given us, both individually and corporately. Let us try to think God's thoughts after Him. Let us attempt to uncover God's strategy--to think about the people to whom we may be called, to earnestly consider their needs, to take into account all that God might do to reach them. Let us make certain that we are clean vessels, fit for His use. And then let us go forward believing that God will be faithful and GIVE HIM THE GLORY.

FINDING GOD'S STRATEGY FOR EVANGELIZATION

The Lord Jesus Christ has commanded His Church to make disciples of every people. This task has been given to His Church, His body. Every Christian in every local church, in every country of the world, is called upon to be a witness to the saving power of Jesus Christ. No matter who we are and where we are, if we claim Jesus as Lord, God's good intention for us is that we should proclaim our faith by what we say and how we live.

The Church is multiplying its witness around the world. As Christians reach out with the compassion of Christ to share the gospel in tens of thousands of situations, they need to understand the people to whom they are called, to uncover God's strategy, God's will and plan, for reaching these people. They need to sense that God is setting them aside to be about His business in a particular part of the world.

There are some obvious questions that can be asked that will help the Holy Spirit to give us the mind of Christ:

1. WHAT PEOPLE DOES GOD WANT US TO REACH?

2. WHAT IS THIS PEOPLE LIKE?

3. WHO SHOULD REACH THEM?

4. HOW SHOULD WE REACH THEM?

5. WHAT WILL BE THE RESULT OF REACHING THEM?

These five steps can be thought of as a planning process. The emphasis is placed on asking the right questions, for as each people is unique before God, so will be the answers to the questions.

The five steps we have just listed are all intertwined: what people we want to reach, what the people are like, the means and methods we would use to reach them, who should reach them, are not questions that can be asked one at a time. That is just not the way we think. Obviously our ability to reach a people will have something to do with which people we try to reach. If we cannot discover God's way of reaching them, then we will have to search for a different people.

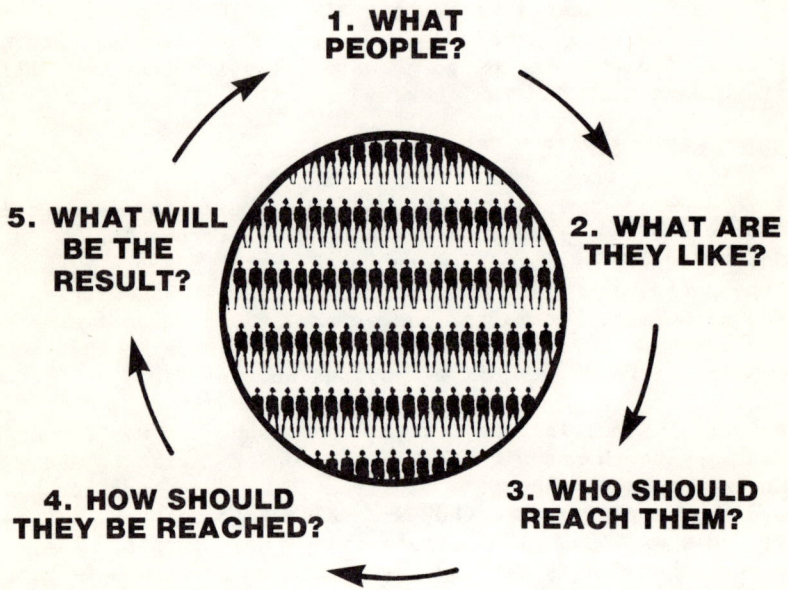

A much better way to think of them would be to see them arranged in a circle. Each question leads to the next, with the last leading back to the first. It is a _process_ that needs to be repeated over and over.

So although the questions are presented in a sequence, you will discover that you will often be asking many different questions at the same time. Don't let the sequence of the questions keep you from allowing the Holy Spirit to lead your mind and heart.

WHAT PEOPLE DOES GOD WANT US TO REACH?

If you believe that God is calling you to be part of His force for evangelization, you may already have sensed the people to whom God is sending you. But suppose that you are an agency, or a local church, or an individual Christian who senses the call of God to evangelize, but does not know where to begin? What should you do?

Go back to the simple chart on page 26 to see what peoples you saw all around you. What does this tell you?

Obtain a copy of the latest edition of the *Unreached Peoples* directory described on page 33. Look through it. Look under the indexes by country, by language, by people, by type of group. What is God saying to you through this information?

In addition, here are some questions that may be helpful to you:

1. *Are there any unreached people groups within your country?*

2. *Are there unreached people groups whose language you already know?*

3. *What special gifts do you and/or your group have for reaching a particular unreached people?*

4. *What successful experience have you or your group had in reaching a particular kind of unreached people?*

You may have to return to these questions after you have looked further in the pages that follow. Sometimes we have to step out in faith and tell the Lord that this is the people we believe He wants us to reach and then go on with the explanation to see whether we really are following the mind of the Spirit.

6

COMING TO KNOW A PEOPLE

It may be the man and wife who are living next door to you. It may be a particular group of people within the city or neighborhood in which we live. It may be a group of people who are living in a distant land. But, regardless of the particular people to whom God has called you to be an evangelist, it is important to understand them within their <u>need</u>. The good news must always be seen and applied within the life and needs of the individual. The gospel transforms societies. The way in which it is communicated and the strategy we use to attempt to reach a particular people should always consider their situation and <u>their</u> need. The place to begin is not with the method of evangelization, but rather with an understanding of the people whom God loves and for whom Christ died.

We need to identify the people to whom God has called us and for the moment to put aside those to whom we are not called. So first we need to establish some kind of definition or boundary for the group we hope to reach. Such boundaries might be geographical. We might decide to consider all the people in our home country, all the people on a given island, or all the people within the city where we live or even the people within a region.

On a smaller scale we may have a very precise group such as a given tribe or our own social group. Here we will want to break the group down into age groups, natural leaders, significant individuals, etc.

By further dividing the people we are trying to reach with the gospel, we will not only make the overall task easier to understand and manage, but we will also discover where different members of the local church or the total force for evangelization can best fit into God's strategy for reaching this people.

But, most important, we can understand where _we_ fit.

FOCUS ON A SPECIAL PEOPLE GROUP

A number of different things contribute to create a distinctive people group, one that in some way shares a common way of life, sees itself as a particular group having an affinity for one another, and differs to some extent from other groups or people. This may be because of shared language, religion, ethnicity, residence, occupation, class, caste, special situation or some combination of these.

Some examples might be French Canadian college students in Montreal, Urdu-speaking Muslim farmers of the Punjab, Chinese refugees from Vietnam living in France, Welsh working class miners, white "swinging singles" in North American apartments. Each shared characteristic helps to unify the group and place "boundaries" around it.

DESCRIBING THE PEOPLE

The more specific we can be in describing the group we believe God wants evangelized, the better able we will be to discover what it will take to do an effective job and where we fit into it all. The following questions have been taken from the questionnaire used by the Strategy Working Group. You will find these questions in another form on the Unreached Peoples Questionnaire on page 85 of this book. If you want a space to fill out the answers, use that questionnaire.

1. *Name of this group or people?*

2. *Alternate name(s) or spellings?*

3. *Country where located?*

4. Approximate population of the group in this country?

5. What makes them different? Why are they a group?

6. What language do they speak?

These are the basic questions that you will need to learn more about the group. But to help you with your research, here are some additional questions that have been found useful by the Strategy Working Group:

7. Names of religious groups found among this people?

8. Percent who are adherents of this religion?

9. Percent who practice this religion?

10. What is the attitude of this people toward Christianity?

11. Which language would you say is most suitable for presentation of the gospel?

12. If there is a Christian witness present, what language(s) is being used?

13. What is the status of Scripture translation in the language you consider most suitable for communicating the gospel?

14. If there are Christian churches or missions (national or foreign) now active within the area or region where this people is concentrated, who are they?

15. In your opinion, what is the attitude of this people to religious change of any kind?

There are two other key questions which everyone needs to ask:

16. What other questions do you think are important for this particular people?

17. Who else could you consult that would have more information about these people or who might have some additional good questions?

LOOKING AT CULTURE

The above questions are a good beginning. But we have to go deeper than that. We have to understand what this people is really like. Sometimes we may not be able to do this until we have actually lived among and studied and learned to love a people ourselves. Other times the answers to our questions can come from research and what others have observed.

Every people, insofar as it is a distinct group, shares a common way of life. It has a distinct <u>culture</u> that affects the way it will understand and respond to Jesus Christ. "Culture" refers to the way in which a people do things together in order to survive and to express their particular beliefs and enjoyment of life. Culture includes the whole way of living and thinking of a people group that unifies and gives the people a sense of identity and dignity.

Evangelization always takes place within and through culture. God's own revelation in the Bible was given in terms of the hearers' own culture. Jesus' words and parables telling us of the Kingdom of God were chosen from the experiences and culture of the Jewish people of Palestine. We spend a great deal of time in Bible study attempting to understand the history and cultures of the Bible so as to hear God's word more clearly.

Every evangelist brings his or her own cultural experience and understanding to the task of evangelization. If the gospel is to be expressed afresh, free from the evangelist's own cultural biases, we need to understand our own biases.

So, too, the culture of the people to be evangelized must be deeply understood and sympathetically appreciated. Learning another culture often takes a lifetime. An adequate description of a people and their culture might take thousands of detailed pages.

The relationship of Christianity and culture has been of deep interest and concern to the Lausanne Committee for World Evangelization. A report of a consultation jointly sponsored by the LCWE Strategy Working Group and Theology and Education Group discusses this in much more detail. This report, known as *The Willowbank Report* is available to you. For more information see page 82.

For an evangelistic strategy two things are crucial: First, what is the potential "fit" between the gospel and the culture of the people? What aspects of the culture will help understanding and make the gospel relevant? Where might there be potential conflict, if the gospel's demands for repentance run opposite the culture?

Second, how well does the current culture meet the needs of the people? Are they satisfied with their current way of life? Or is there discontent and a searching for something new, that the Christian faith would answer? How receptive might the people be to religious change of any kind or to the gospel? The following questions will help you understand better:

18. *What cultural values, beliefs, practices of the people might* help *them understand the gospel and feel favorable toward it?*

    For example, if the people have strong positive feelings about the importance of the family, the gospel's emphasis on the family would be a bridge to them.

19. *What cultural values, beliefs, practices of the people might* hinder *their understanding or feeling favorable toward the gospel?*

    For example, if the people practice polygamy they might feel negative towards the gospel which calls for marriage to one wife.

20. *Are there some common cultural practices that seem to be clearly prohibited by Scripture? If so, what are they?*

    For example, the people might worship a number of different gods who are seen to perform different acts for them.

21. *Are there some common, important cultural values or practices which could be reinterpreted and incorporated into a new Christian lifestyle? If so, what are they?*

    For example, a group of people might have a strong feeling of community responsibility which would fit well into the biblical concept of "the body of Christ."

22. *Do the people find genuine satisfaction from their traditional religious or magical practices in the face of disease, sickness or death? What seems*

to make them content or discontent with their current religious involvement?

WHERE ARE THEY IN THEIR MOVEMENT TOWARD CHRIST?

On page 39 of this report we discussed how every people group is in movement towards Christ. Obviously not everyone in a group will necessarily be at the same point at the same time. But if we are to select the right means and methods of evangelism, as we discuss on page 65, then it is very helpful to know where most of the people of this unreached people group are.

Here are the different steps that we described on pages 40 and 41. Next to each one put in your estimate of the approximate number of people who might be at this point. Accuracy is not important. You're only trying to get a general idea. But this description, this profile, can be very useful to you.

Movement Toward Christ		Your Rough Estimate as to How Many People are at Each Place
No Awareness of Christianity	-7	
Awareness of the Existence of Christianity	-6	
Some Knowledge of the Gospel	-5	
Understanding of the Fundamentals of the Gospel	-4	
Grasp of the Personal Implications	-3	
Recognition of Personal Need	-2	
Challenge and Decision to Receive Christ	-1	
Evaluation of the Decision	+1	
Incorporation into a Fellowship of Christians	+2	
Active Propagators of the Gospel	+3	

7

WHO SHOULD REACH THEM?

THE FORCE FOR EVANGELIZATION

It is very easy for one to start thinking about evangelizing a particular group and to overlook the fact that there may be many other members of the body of Christ who also may be interested or may be of help in reaching this people. We call all of these people the "force for evangelization." It might include the existing Christians who are within the group community or location, the organized church there, other Christian organizations working there, or organizations outside the area who might have a potential interest in this group.

If there is a local church, then we need to consult with the church leaders there. We need to find out what <u>they</u> think needs to be done or what they are doing. We need to ask about evangelists from other parts of the country or missionaries from some other countries. In short, we need to try to get an overall picture of what God is doing through the <u>total body of Christ</u>.

Analyze which churches are growing and attracting converts and which are not. <u>Why</u> is this true? What is it about those that appear to be effective that we can learn? When did they start to grow?

We also need to be aware that the force <u>for</u> evangelization is always faced with forces <u>opposed</u> to evangelization. The Church grows in the midst of and in spite of various groups and pressures that seek to hinder the progress of the gospel.

OBTAINING INFORMATION

For more information on what might be going on within a city, people, state or country, look for church handbooks that may be published, government statistics, lists of organizations who have been authorized by the government to work in these areas, Status of Christianity profiles published by SWG/MARC for a particular country, and specific local groups such as chambers of commerce, labor unions, council of churches, and mission associations.

Do your homework! This information is much easier to get than it may seem.

Personal mail or telephone inquiries to Christian organizations and churches that you know about who may be working in this area asking <u>them</u> who they might know about will also be very profitable.

QUESTIONS TO ASK

Here are some questions that can help.

1. *What churches, agencies, or other groups of Christians are already working with these people? What are they doing? How effective, in your opinion, have they been?*

2. *Which groups or agencies appear to understand the basic need of this people?*

3. *If there are already churches established, which, if any, have shown significant growth (50 percent) in the last five years? Why?*

4. Are the established churches accepted as culturally part of the group? Why?

5. Who appear to be the key Christians or Christian groups to reach this people?

6. Where can we get more accurate information about the possible force for evangelization?

While you are thinking about the force for evangelization, it is a good time to be thinking about forces that will be opposed to evangelization. Here are some questions that may be helpful.

7. What organized groups or agencies would be opposed to the proclamation of the gospel among this group?

8. What forces, spiritual or other, appear to be arrayed against the gospel? What forces hinder individuals or family groups from committing themselves to Christ in an open and active way?

9. If some have become Christians and then turned away from the Lord, what were the things that seemed important in drawing them away from God?

10. If Christians are present in this group, what important factors, if any, seem to keep them from active and effective witness?

8

HOW SHOULD THEY BE REACHED?

Each individual comes to know Jesus Christ as a personal experience. The Person of our Lord meets the <u>person</u> in a one-to-one relationship. However, within different cultures, societies, situations, different means and methods of communicating the gospel have been found effective. There is a danger that we will adopt one method and believe that this method is always useful for all different peoples in all different situations. This is obviously not so.

We have an infinite God. He is capable of an infinite variety of means and methods to reach people. We need to be ready to accept this marvelous diversity.

At the same time, through the history of Christ's Church, we have learned a great deal about how people come to know Christ. There are "methods" and "means" of all types available: door-to-door visitation, street corner witnessing, radio broadcasts, cassette ministries, literature distribution, evangelistic meetings, church services and a host of others. These need to be evaluated both as to their initial impact and their lasting results.

Earlier we mentioned how part of our task is to design a key to especially open the door to the particular people to whom God has called us. In most cases this key will be made up of many different types of evangelistic methods. But as we examine and accept or reject various methods of evangelization or forge new ones from parts of others, we should be careful not to give the impression that we are making an overall value judgment about any of them. The means or method that works well in middle-class U.S.A. may be completely out of place in middle-class Brazil. Literature that was just right for the urbanite may have no place in rural evangelism.

In all of this we need to be particularly sensitive to what this people already knows about the gospel.

QUESTIONS TO ASK

1. In light of the needs of this people, where they seem to be as a group in their understanding of the gospel, the particular cultural factors making them responsive or resistant, the available force for evangelization, and forces opposed, what means and methods do we believe most likely to meet the need?

2. Will these methods move the people toward Christ? When will the methods have to be changed because the people *have* moved?

3. Do these suggested methods conform to biblical principles? Are they biblically ethical?

4. Where could we learn more about possible means or methods?

5. What organizations or individuals will probably cooperate with us?

6. *Can the previously identified force for evangelization carry out these means and methods? If not, should the methods or the evangelists be changed?*

YOUR STRATEGY

7. *Write a paragraph which explains what part or subgroup of the people you will begin with, what need you propose to meet, who will be involved as the force for evangelization, how the forces opposed will be met, and what means and methods will be used.*

9

WHAT WILL BE THE RESULT?

No one can predict the future. God is still in control of the universe, and His will will be done. Evidently God expects us to exercise our faith in deciding what He would have us to be, where He would have us to go and what He would have us to do. He expects us to think about the future, to discover the directions our lives should take. He expects us to think about the outcomes, or goals, of the activities in which we are going to become involved.

In order for such outcomes to be useful, they need to be <u>measurable</u>. It is good to have an overall purpose to evangelize the people of our city. But unless we define what we mean by "evangelize," unless we decide how many people, and what people we are talking about, unless we think about what we expect to happen as a result of our evangelistic activity, we may very well be working with no way to communicate with each other about what we hope to do, and no assurance as to whether we are reaching the goals to which God has pointed us.

All this means is that we must be able to know <u>whether</u> and <u>when</u> the outcome we anticipated or the goal we set has actually occurred. So we avoid such vague outcomes or goals as: "to have large attendance" at evangelistic meetings, "many conversions" through the correspondence course, "rapid" church growth. Instead we state by faith how many people we think God might bring to the meetings, how many might be converted, what percentage of growth is expected for a given period of time. Clear, measurable outcomes are a mark of effective strategy and a working faith.

We need to state <u>how we will know</u> whether it has happened or not so that we can build on the results. Only when we have told one another what we expect to happen can we begin to evaluate the direction we are going and how effective are our methods in reaching the goals God has given us.

QUESTIONS TO ASK

1. *If your approach is successful, what do you expect God to do? What do you think God will allow the force for evangelization to accomplish?*

2. *How will you describe where this people is in their movement towards Christ? What will be the evidence?*

3. *How will you know whether it happened or not so you can build on the results? What will be the measurement?*

4. *What problems will you encounter with this approach? How can you minimize or overcome them?*

THE RESULTING CHURCH

One of the most important outcomes will be Christians entering into the fellowship of a local congregation. In some situations it will mean developing completely new congregations. In other situations, new Christians will be brought into the fellowship of previously existing congregations.

On the basis of what you know about the people's culture, what should that church be like? How might Christianity be made dynamic and vital among this people? What kind of church will new converts have to become a part of? Will your strategy produce such a church?

Here are some other questions to help your thinking and praying:

5. If members of this group became Christians, what kind of a biblical, worshipping fellowship would be most likely to attract other members of the same group?

6. What means of worship do you think they will use?

7. How will the people of this church demonstrate concern for one another?

8. What means of witness will they use to bring others into a knowledge of Christ?

9. Is this the type of fellowship which is available or which we expect to result from our strategy? If not, how do our means and methods, the force for evangelization, or strategy need to be changed to bring about a more satisfactory fellowship of Christians?

GOALS FOR EVANGELIZATION

You earlier stated what you expected God to do as a result of your actions. These were anticipated outcomes, some good and some not so good. Some were measurable. Others were not. Now, for each desired outcome you need to state what will have to happen for it to come to pass. What goals or steps are needed?

As you write your goal statements, remember they need to be specific, achievable and measurable.

10. *What are the goals or steps that God wants to see happen with this people?*

PLANS FOR EVANGELIZATION

Each goal needs a plan for action. We have made up a worksheet to help you on page 73. Number the goals. Copy this page in some way so that you have one worksheet for each of your goals. When you have stated what you plan to accomplish, when it will happen, how you can measure that it has happened, the steps necessary, who is responsible and how much it will cost, you will have a plan you can share with one another and offer as your statement of faith to God as to what you believe He would have you do. If you need more help in planning, see Chapter 10.

GOAL NAME _____   GOAL NUMBER _____

PURPOSE   For this reason: _____
                                _____
                                _____
                                _____

GOAL   We plan to   _____
          accomplish
          this: _____

                                _____

          by this date: _____

          We will know it   _____
          has happened
          because: _____

STEPS   We plan to   _____
          take these
          steps: _____

                                _____

                                _____

                                _____

PEOPLE   These people   _____
          are responsible:
                                _____

COST   It will cost   _____
          this amount:

RESOURCES NEEDED TO CARRY OUT THE PLAN

Plans won't work if we don't have the resources to carry them out. Resources include the various people who are going to be needed, the financial support that may be required, the various tools, such as radio, literature, recordings, etc., the prayer support that is needed to undergird all of this. Look at each step of your plan. What resources are going to be needed for each step? What cooperation are you going to need from other groups?

What people, how much money, and what other resources, such as other organizations and churches, are needed to carry out these plans? List them for each of your goals, and then add them up.

RESOURCES FOR EVANGELIZATION			
GOAL	PEOPLE	MONEY	TOOLS

BEFORE WE BEGIN

We have identified the people to whom we believe God has called us. We have listed those whom God might provide to try to reach them. We have tried to set down a plan as to how we might reach a given people whom we believe need the message of the gospel. We have taken into account where they are, their moving toward Christ, and we have analyzed all the resources that might be needed. But before we begin, we need to ask some final prayerful questions. Go through the steps of the strategy cycle in your mind again:

What does this tell you? Did you consider each step?

Is the plan practical? Do we really have the faith to believe that this is God's best for us? If not, what next? How should we modify what we have done so far? Go back and review again. Prayerfully consider each assumption that you have made.

Does the plan fit your strategy?

If the plan looks like God's best, what is our first step?

> So then, my dear brothers, stand firm and steady. Keep busy always in your work for the Lord, since you know that nothing you do in the Lord's service is ever without value (1 Corinthians 15:58, TEV).

10

FOR FURTHER HELP

THE POWER AND PRESENCE OF PRAYER

On page 48 we discussed the mysteries that surround evangelization. God is doing it all, yet we are responsible. We need to plan, but it is the Holy Spirit who will ultimately decide what needs to be done. In order to be led by God's Spirit we need to be in communication with Him. It is not a question of planning and then praying and then planning some more. Rather it is a question of surrounding everything we do with prayer. In order to experience the power of prayer, prayer must be present in all that we do.

STUDY GROUPS

In preparation for the Consultation on World Evangelization at Pattaya, Thailand, in June 1980, the Lausanne Committee for World Evangelization has appointed a number of Coordinators to select Conveners of study groups in different parts of the world. The areas that these Coordinators are covering are:

Study Group

1. Reaching Traditional Religionists:

    a. *Africa*

       b. *Asia and Oceania*

       c. *Latin America and Caribbean*

       d. *Non-Literates*

2. Reaching Buddhists

3. Reaching Mystics and Cultists

4. Reaching Hindus

5. Reaching Jews

6. Reaching Marxists

7. Reaching Secularists

8. Reaching Muslims (jointly sponsored with WEF)

9. Reaching Chinese

10. <u>Reaching City-Dwellers</u>:

       a. Inner-City

       b. Large City (Conurbations)

11. <u>Reaching Nominal Christians</u>:

       a. Among Roman Catholics

       b. Among Orthodox

       c. Among Protestants

For information on study groups on unreached people that are being convened in your part of the world, write to the Coordinator of your interest group, or send your name to the Lausanne Committee for World Evangelization, P.O. Box 21225, Nairobi, Kenya, East Africa, or to the COWE Program office, P.O. Box 1179, Wheaton, Illinois 60187, U.S.A., and they will have the Coordinator get in touch with you.

These study groups will be forwarding to the 1980 Consultation the insight that people like yourself will be contributing.

AUDIOVISUAL FOR YOUR USE

Under the guidance of the Strategy Working Group, MARC has prepared an audiovisual entitled "That Everyone May Hear." Much of the information in this book is covered by the audiovisual which has been designed as a study tool. The audiovisual kit includes a 30 minute cassette tape, 130 slides (35 mm) or a filmstrip, a copy of the script in English with the number of the pictures keyed to the script, and directions for its use.

"That Everyone May Hear" is being supplied in limited quantities by the Strategy Working Group to the Coordinators at no charge. Additional copies are available from MARC at 919 West Huntington Drive, Monrovia, California 91016, U.S.A. See the order form on the rear of this book.

The pictures used in the presentation have been drawn from all the areas of the world. Where diagrams and written words are used they have been done in English. It is anticipated that many will want to translate the script into their language, making necessary cultural adaptations and record it again, so that it can be used in many different language settings. It is also possible, of course, to change some of the slides to make them more suitable for presentation in your local region. Of course, using the filmstrip makes it impossible to change the pictures.

Before translating the script or making up new slides, we suggest that you write to MARC asking whether others have already done so. For example, the script and tape is already available in Spanish.

TO HELP YOU DISCOVER UNREACHED PEOPLES

Since the 1974 Lausanne Conference the Status of Christianity Country Profiles have been revised and updated. The following Country Profiles are available in English:

Asia

Afghanistan
Bangladesh
Burma
Burma-Karen People
Cambodia
Hong Kong
India
   Andhra Pradesh
   Arunachal Pradesh
   Assam
   Gujarat
Indonesia
Japan
Korea
Laos
Macao
Pakistan
Philippines
Singapore
Sri Lanka
Taiwan
Thailand

Asia (Continued)

Vietnam
Malaysia

Africa

Burundi	Liberia
Egypt	North Africa
Ethiopia	South Africa
Ghana	Sudan
Kenya	Swaziland

Europe

Finland	Norway
France	Portugal
Greece	Spain

Latin America

Argentina	Haiti
Bolivia	Mexico
Brazil	Panama
Colombia	Puerto Rico
Ecuador	

North America

Canada
Hawaii
U.S.A.

Oceania

Oceania (General)
Australia
Fiji-Indians
New Zealand
Papua New Guinea

These Country Profiles are six-to-eight page descriptions of a country, giving a brief historical background which emphasizes Christianity and giving the current size of the church and Christian agencies working within the country. The status of unreached peoples is also described.

Country Profiles have been packaged in book form of different areas of the world. Under the title of *World Christianity* groups of Status of Christianity Country Profiles with detailed information on unreached people are available for the following areas of the world:

Name	Date Available
Middle East	June 11, 1979
Eastern Asia	August 31, 1979
South Asia	November 30, 1979
Latin America	February 29, 1980

In order to obtain either the individual profiles or copies of *World Christianity*, use the publication order form at the back of this book.

INFORMATION ON UNREACHED PEOPLE

The David C. Cook Company publishes an annual directory entitled *Unreached Peoples*. *Unreached Peoples '79* was the first of this series. *Unreached Peoples '80* will be available in December 1979. Hundreds of unreached peoples groups around the world are listed. In addition, some eighty-to-ninety are described in greater detail in each directory.

If you wish to get a copy of *Unreached Peoples '79*, use the publication order form at the back of the book.

If you would like to discover whether information on a particular unreached people is available, write to MARC, 919 W. Huntington Drive, Monrovia, California 91016, U.S.A.

If you would like to have information on the unreached people that you know of included in the next copy of the directory, and/or made available for the 1980 Consultation on World Evangelization, send the completed questionnaire on page 85 to MARC at the address noted above.

INSIGHTS INTO CULTURE

The "Homogeneous Unit Principle" has been an outgrowth of a developing understanding of how churches grow. It helps us understand the way the gospel spread along the natural culture lines with a homogeneous group of people. This sociological understanding was reviewed in depth by a consultation sponsored by the Lausanne Theology and Education Group during June, 1977. The helpful report on this consultation is included in Lausanne Occasional Paper No. 1 - *The Pasadena Consultation*.

In January, 1978, a study group convened jointly by the Theology and Education Group and the Strategy Working Group produced Lausanne Occasional Paper No. 2, *The Willowbank Report - Gospel and Culture*. This extremely informative booklet covers a wide range of topics that deal with the interaction between the gospel and culture. Both these reports are available from either MARC or Lausanne Committee for World Evangelization, P.O. Box 1100, Wheaton, Illinois 60187, U.S.A.; or P.O. Box 21225, Nairobi, Kenya; or 19 Draycott Place, London SW3 ZSJ England; or P.O. Box 337, Tanglin Post Office, Singapore 10. See the publication order form.

INSIGHTS INTO BASIS FOR EVANGELIZATION

At the close of the International Congress on World Evangelization, a covenant was drafted and signed by a large number of those in attendance. This Lausanne Covenant has been the foundation upon which the ongoing work of the Lausanne Committee for World Evangelization has been based. The Reverend John Stott has produced an insightful commentary on the Lausanne Covenant, which, along with the Covenant, has been published as Lausanne Occasional Paper No. 3. It too is available from the addresses noted above or through the publication order form in this book.

MUSLIM EVANGELIZATION

For those who have a particular concern to share Christ with Muslims there is a fourth Lausanne paper: *The Glen Eyrie Report*. During October 1978 approximately 150 people interested in Muslim evangelization met in Colorado Springs to examine strategies for reaching Muslims. This report gives an overview of theif findings. It too is available from the above addresses.

TO HELP YOU IN PLANNING

Many people have little experience in some of the simple mechanics of planning and goal setting. A book that has been widely used throughout the world to help Christian organizations understand both goal setting and planning is *God's Purpose/Man's Plans*. This 59 page book is available from MARC. See the publication order form.

Much of the material in *That Everyone May Hear* has been condensed from the workbook *Planning Strategies for Evangelism*. Most of the questions included in *Planning Strategies for Evangelism* have been included in this book. However, many people have found that *Planning Strategies for Evangelism*, an 8½ x 11" workbook, is most useful when working together with groups. Copies may be ordered through the publication order form.

FINDING THE UNREACHED: YOU CAN HELP!

You can help locate unreached people groups

You are part of a worldwide network of concerned Christians. There are millions upon millions of people in the world who have had little or no contact with the gospel of Jesus Christ. Because of this, we are asking you to help the Church locate and identify these peoples so it can reach them.

Within each country there are distinct and unique groups of people who may be unreached. This questionnaire is designed to help you describe such groups so that Christians everywhere may pray and consider how these groups might be reached with the gospel. This information will be continuously compiled and made available to the Church and her mission agencies. It appears each year in an annual directory, *Unreached Peoples,* produced by David C. Cook.

There are many different groups of people in the world. How varied they are! Consequently, this questionnaire may not always ask the best questions for understanding a particular people. The questions have been asked in a way that will give comparative information to as large a number of Christians as possible. Where you feel another form of question would better suit your situation, please feel free to comment.

What is a "people group"?

A people group is a part of a society that has some basic characteristics in common that cause it to feel a sense of oneness, and set it apart from other groups. It may be unified by language, religion, economic status, occupation, ethnic origin, geographic location, or social position. For example, a distinct group based on ethnic, language and geographic characteristics might be the Quechua of Bolivia; a sociological group might be the urban university and college students of Colombia, or the urban industrial workers of France. It is important to see that groups may share a common way of life and sense of oneness because of social, occupational or economic characteristics, as well as because of language or ethnic origin. Therefore, whenever possible, *describe the smallest number of persons who make up a distinct group;* that is, don't say that all persons in a region or province are a group, rather describe the specific subgroups within that region or province.

Who are the "unreached and unevangelized people"?

Christians have different definitions of the terms "unreached" or "unevangelized." For the purposes of this worldwide effort, we describe an unreached or unevangelized people as a people who has not received or responded to the gospel. This unresponsiveness may be due to lack of opportunity, to lack of understanding, or because the people has not received enough information about the gospel message in its own language through the eyes of its own culture so that it can truly respond to Christ.

We consider a people "unreached" when less than 20 percent of the members of the group are *practicing* Christians, that is, are active members of the Christian community. By "Christian" we mean adherents (church members, families and followers) of the historic Christian communions; Protestant, Anglican, Roman Catholic, Orthodox and such independent groups as may claim the Bible as the basis of faith and Jesus Christ as Lord and Savior. A group less than 20 percent Christian may yet need Christians from outside the group to help with the evangelism task.

How you can provide information

The attached questionnaire has two parts. If you only have information for the first part, send that in now.

Please fill in one questionnaire for *each* people group with which you are familiar. Do not put several groups on one questionnaire. (If you need more questionnaires, ask for extra copies or photocopy this one, or typewrite the questions you are answering on a separate sheet of paper.) We realize that one person may not have all the answers to these questions. Just answer what you can. PLEASE DO NOT WAIT UNTIL YOU HAVE ALL THE INFORMATION REQUESTED ON THIS QUESTIONNAIRE. SEND WHAT YOU HAVE. Other people may provide information that you do not have. Thank you for your help!

When you have completed this questionnaire, please return it to:

Unreached Peoples Program Director
c/o MARC, 919 W. Huntington Drive, Monrovia, CA 91016 U.S.A.

SURVEY QUESTIONNAIRE FOR UNEVANGELIZED AND UNREACHED PEOPLES

Do you see a group of people who are unreached or unevangelized? Identify them! As the Lord spoke to Ezekiel of old, so He speaks to us today. "Son of man, What do you see"?

Answers to the questions on these two pages will provide the minimum information needed to list this people group in the *Unreached Peoples* annual.

After you have read the directions, type or print your answers so they can be easily read. It is unlikely that you will have all the information requested. Do the best you can. What information you are lacking others may supply. If your information is a best guess or estimate, merely place an "E" after it. Send in what you have as soon as possible. Please ignore the small numbers next to the answers. They help others prepare your answers for the *Unreached Peoples* annual.

"For this reason I bow my knees before the Father, from whom every family in heaven and on earth is named . . ."
Ephesians 3:14-15 (RSV)

1. Name of the group or people: _____
2. Alternate name(s) or spelling: _____
3. Country where located: _____
4. Approximate size of the group in this country: _____
5. Vernacular or common language: _____
6. Lingua franca or trade language: _____
7. Name of religious groups found among this people:

CHRISTIAN GROUPS:	% who are adherents of this religion	% who practice this religion
Protestant	_____ %	_____ %
Roman Catholic	_____ %	_____ %
Eastern Orthodox	_____ %	_____ %
Other Christian: _____ (name)	_____ %	_____ %
NON-CHRISTIAN GROUPS OR SECULARISM:		
_____	_____ %	_____ %
_____	_____ %	_____ %
_____	_____ %	_____ %
_____	_____ %	_____ %
TOTAL FOR ALL GROUPS:	100 %	

"Brethren, My heart's desire and prayer to God for them is that they may be saved."
Romans 10:1 (RSV)

PLEASE TEAR OFF INSTRUCTIONS BEFORE MAILING

8. In your opinion, what is the attitude of this people toward Christianity?

(01)☐ Strongly favorable   (02)☐ Somewhat favorable   (03)☐ Indifferent   (04)☐ Somewhat opposed   (05)☐ Strongly opposed

TURN THIS SHEET OVER FOR PAGE 2

9. Questionnaire completed by:

   Name: _____ Date: _____

   Organization: _____

   Address: _____

   _____

10. Who else might be able to provide information about this people?

Name	Organization (if any)	Address

11. If you are aware of any publications describing this people, please give title and author.

    _____

12. What other information do you have that could help others to understand this people better? What do you feel would help in evangelizing them? *(Use additional sheet if necessary.)*

"And how are they to believe in him of whom they have never heard? And how are they to hear without a preacher?"
Romans 10:14 (RSV)

13. Are you also sending in pages 3 and 4? ☐ Yes ☐ No

Please send whatever information you have immediately. Do not wait until you have every answer.

Mail to:

Unreached Peoples Program Director
c/o MARC, 919 W. Huntington Drive, Monrovia, CA 91016 USA

Name of people group described_____ Your name _____ Date _____

If you have any more information about this people group, please complete the following two pages as best you can. If not, please send in pages one and two now. If you can obtain more information later, send it in as soon as possible.

PEOPLE DISTINCTIVES—What makes them different? Why are they a people group?

14. A number of different things contribute to create a distinctive people or group, one that in some way shares a common way of life, *sees* itself as a particular group having an affinity toward one another, and differs to some extent from other groups or peoples. What would you say makes the people you are describing distinctive? Check the appropriate box of as many of the following descriptions as *are important* in making this people distinctive. Use the following scale: "High" importance, "Medium" importance, "Low" importance. For example, if you thought that the fact that they had a common political loyalty was of medium importance in unifying and making a group distinctive, you would place an "X" in the middle box under "Medium".

Importance — High / Medium / Low

- (01) ☐ ☐ ☐ Same language
- (02) ☐ ☐ ☐ Common political loyalty
- (03) ☐ ☐ ☐ Similar occupation
- (04) ☐ ☐ ☐ Racial or ethnic similarity
- (05) ☐ ☐ ☐ Shared religious customs
- (06) ☐ ☐ ☐ Common kinship ties
- (07) ☐ ☐ ☐ Strong sense of unity
- (08) ☐ ☐ ☐ Similar education level
- (09) ☐ ☐ ☐ Other(s) _____ *(please write in)*

Importance — High / Medium / Low

- (10) ☐ ☐ ☐ Common residential area
- (11) ☐ ☐ ☐ Similar social class or caste
- (12) ☐ ☐ ☐ Similar economic status
- (13) ☐ ☐ ☐ Shared hobby or special interest
- (14) ☐ ☐ ☐ Discrimination from other groups
- (15) ☐ ☐ ☐ Unique health situation
- (16) ☐ ☐ ☐ Distinctive legal status
- (17) ☐ ☐ ☐ Similar age
- (18) ☐ ☐ ☐ Common significant problems

15. How rapidly would you say the lifestyle of this people is changing? (check one)

(01) ☐ Very Slow Change   (02) ☐ Slow Change   (03) ☐ Moderate Change   (04) ☐ Rapid Change   (05) ☐ Very Rapid Change

"And to him was given dominion and glory and kingdom, that all peoples, nations, and languages should serve him." Daniel 7:14 (RSV)

PEOPLE LANGUAGES—What do they speak?

Please list the various languages used by the members of this people:

LANGUAGE TYPE	Primary name(s) of their language(s)	Approximate % who *speak* this language	Approximate % of people over 15 years of age who *read* this language
16. Vernacular or common language:		____ %	____ %
17. Lingua franca or trade language:		____ %	____ %
18. Language used for instruction in schools:		____ %	____ %
19. Language suitable for presentation of the gospel:		____ %	____ %

20. If there is Christian witness at present, what language(s) is being used? _____

21. Place an "x" in the boxes that indicate the status of Scripture translation *in the language you consider most suitable for communicating the gospel* (question 19):

	CURRENT STATUS			AVAILABLE		
	Not available	In process	Completed	In oral form	In print	On cassette or records
(POR) New Testament portions	☐	☐	☐	☐	☐	☐
(NT) Complete New Testament	☐	☐	☐	☐	☐	☐
(OT) Complete Old Testament	☐	☐	☐	☐	☐	☐

22. Of the <u>Christians</u> present among this people, what percent *over 15 years of age can* and *do read any language?*

_____ %

CHRISTIAN WITNESS TO THIS PEOPLE—Who is trying to reach them?

23. If there are Christian churches or missions (national or foreign) now active *within the area or region where this people is concentrated,* please give the following information:
    (If there are none, check here: ☐)

CHURCH OR MISSION Name of church, denomination	YEAR Year work began in this area	MEMBERS Approximate number of full members from this people	ADHERENTS Approximate number of adherents (community including children)	WORKERS Approximate numbers of trained pastors and evangelists from this people
_____	_____	_____	_____	_____
_____	_____	_____	_____	_____

"... with an eternal gospel to proclaim to those who dwell on earth, to every nation and tribe and tongue, and people."
Revelation 14:6 (RSV)

24. What is the growth rate of the total Christian community among this people group?

    (01)☐ Rapid growth   (02)☐ Slow growth   (03)☐ Stable   (04)☐ Slow decline   (05)☐ Rapid decline

25. In your opinion, what is the attitude of this people to religious change of any kind?

    (01)☐ Very open   (02)☐ Somewhat open   (03)☐ Indifferent   (04)☐ Somewhat closed   (05)☐ Very closed

26. In your opinion, what is the attitude of this people toward Christianity?

    (01)☐ Strongly favorable   (02)☐ Somewhat favorable   (03)☐ Indifferent   (04)☐ Somewhat opposed   (05)☐ Strongly opposed

27. Most people move through a series of more or less well-defined stages in their attitude toward Christianity. Parts of a people group will be further along than other parts. Here are ten categories that attempt to show this progression. However, locating people in some of these categories can be difficult, so to make things simpler some categories are combined in the questions that follow.

    In your estimation, what percentage of this people can be described as those who: (These percentages are exclusive. Do not include people more than once. Your total should add up to 100%.)

"And you he made alive when you were dead, through the trespasses and sins in which you once walked..."
Ephesians 2:1-2 (RSV)

Have no awareness of Christianity .... _____ %

Have awareness of the existence of Christianity .... _____ %

Have some knowledge of the gospel .... _____ %

Understand the message of the gospel .... _____ %

See the personal implications of the gospel ....⎫

Recognize a personal need that the gospel can meet ....⎬ _____ %

Are being challenged to receive Christ ....⎭

Have decided for Christ, but are not incorporated into a fellowship
(may be evaluating their decision) .... _____ %

Are incorporated into a fellowship of Christians .... _____ %

Are active propagators of the gospel .... _____ %

                                                      TOTAL   100 %

28. On the whole, how accurate is the information you have given us?

    (V)☐ Very accurate   (F)☐ Fairly accurate   (E)☐ Good estimate   (G)☐ Mainly guesses

29. Are you willing to have your name publically associated with this information?

    ☐ No   ☐ Yes   ☐ Yes, with qualifications: _____

PUBLICATION ORDER FORM

	No. Each	Unit Price	Total Price
INDIVIDUAL COUNTRY PROFILES (see over)			
_____	____	$ .60	____
_____	____	$ .60	____
_____	____	$ .60	____
_____	____	$ .60	____
WORLD CHRISTIANITY			
Middle East	____	$ 6.00	____
Eastern Asia - available Aug. 31, 1979	____	$ 6.00	____
South Asia - available Nov. 30, 1979	____	$ 6.00	____
Latin America - available Feb. 29, 1980	____	$	____
LAUSANNE OCCASIONAL PAPERS			
The Pasadena Consultation	____	$ 1.00	____
The Willowbank Report	____	$ 1.00	____
The Lausanne Covenant	____	$ 1.00	____
The Glen Eyrie Report	____	$ 1.00	____
PLANNING STRATEGIES FOR EVANGELISM	____	$ 2.00	____
THAT EVERYONE MAY HEAR	____	$ 2.50	____
THAT EVERYONE MAY HEAR - Audiovisual			
Slides and cassette tape	____	$ 40.00	____
Filmstrip and cassette tape	____	$ 40.00	____
UNREACHED PEOPLES DIRECTORY			
Unreached Peoples '79	____	$ 4.50	____
Unreached Peoples '80 - available Dec. 1979	____	$	____

*All prices have been reduced to the discounted single copy price.

SUBTOTAL (MINIMUM ORDER $2.00) _____

Note: California residents please add 6% sales tax. _____

☐ Payment included (postpaid). **TOTAL** _____
☐ Bill me—POSTAGE PLUS 10% HANDLING ($1.00 min., $5.00 max.)

POSTAGE AND HANDLING _____

In **Canada**, order from:
Communication and Services Division
World Vision of Canada
6630 Turner Valley Road
Mississauga, Ont. L5N 2S4, Canada

In **Europe**, order from:
Evangelical Missionary Alliance
19 Draycott Place
London SW3 2SJ, England

Please make checks payable to MARC/World Vision.
All orders must be remitted in U.S. funds because of the high cost of currency exchange.

TOTAL _____

THE PRICES LISTED ARE VALID THROUGH DECEMBER 1979 ONLY.

Listing of individual country profiles available at 60¢ each:

ASIA
Afghanistan
Bangladesh
Burma
Burma-Karen People
Cambodia
Hong Kong
India (General)
  Andhra Pradesh
  Arunachal Pradesh
  Assam
  Gujarat
Indonesia
Japan
Korea
Laos
Macao
Pakistan
Philippines
Singapore
Sri Lanka
Taiwan
Thailand
Vietnam
Malaysia

AFRICA
Burundi
Egypt
Ethiopia
Ghana
Kenya
Liberia
North Africa
South Africa
Sudan
Swaziland

EUROPE
Finland
France
Greece
Norway
Portugal
Spain

LATIN AMERICA
Argentina
Bolivia
Brazil
Colombia
Ecuador
Haiti
Mexico
Panama
Puerto Rico

NORTH AMERICA
Canada
Hawaii (USA)
U.S.A.

OCEANIA
Oceania (General)
Australia
Fiji-Indians
New Zealand
Papua New Guinea

The World

List the profiles you want on the other side.

_____
Your Name

_____
Address

_____
City, State, Zip

_____
Organization

Mail to: MARC
919 West Huntington Drive
Monrovia, California 91916 U.S.A.